DHCC PRAYER BOOK

Pockets Prayers for Divine Increase

Dr. Pepper Martin & DHCC Life
Application Class Students

RELENTLESS
PUBLISHING

DHCC Prayer Book : Pockets Prayers for Divine Increase

Copyright © 2019 by Dr. Pepper Martin & DHCC Life Application Class Students

Published by :

Relentless Publishing House, LLC

www.relentlesspublishing.com

ISBN: 978-1-948829-25-0

First Edition: May 2019

10 9 8 7 6 5 4 3 2 1

TABLE OF CONTENTS

PREFACE 4

DEBT FORGIVENESS PRAYER 7

GOD'S PROVISION PRAYER...17

FINANCIAL RESPONSIBILITY PRAYER 16

GIVING PRAYER..21

GREED FORGIVENESS PRAYER 25

PREFACE

Destiny House Christian Center is a contemporary, non-denominational church, with traditional values that uses biblical principles as a vehicle to create and develop Spirit-filled disciples of Jesus and help them discover and fulfill their divine purpose to become well-equipped and well-balanced Christians, who serve as living testimonies of hope both globally and within their local communities. Our mission is to create and develop Spirit-filled disciples of Jesus using biblical principles as the vehicle for growth. We help every person discover and fulfill their divine purpose to become well-equipped and well-balanced Christians. Our vision is to be a place where people worship God by discovering their passion, fulfilling their destiny and living their dream through the expression of music, arts and the preaching and teaching of the Word of God.

Our Motto Is: *"We Will Get You Where You Need To Go, Riding On The Word Of God."*

Every Tuesday night, from September to June, we have Life Application Class which consists of mini Bible Classes offering sessions every six weeks. One mini-course offered is entitled "Prayer and Praise Power." This course offers learners in-depth insight on how prayer and praise work together as critical spiritual weapons equipping Christians with the power they need to defeat the kingdom of darkness. Another mini-course is "Money Matters." This course offers learners a biblical prospective on finances and the importance of financial health and its connection to spiritual health, showing "giving" as a form of worship and a fundamental necessity in the life of a Christian.

Our church members immediately began to apply some significant prayer and praise strategies learned in our classes offered on Tuesdays during our weekly Wednesday night intercessory prayer sessions where we pray corporately for the needs of our church members and the needs of the residents of the community. During one Wednesday night prayer, I was inspired by God to have our Life Application Class learners divide into four groups of 5. They assembled in small collaborative prayer groups to write prayers that specifically focused on financial topics previously discussed in our "Money Matters" course. The purpose was to offer prayers written by the congregation that were power-packed, spiritually uplifting and engaging that ministered to all who would read them and bless their families. These prayers dealt with an array of common issues including excessive debt, poverty, over-spending, greed, selfishness and fear.

The entire experience was absolutely incredible! It brought the members of DHCC, who participated, closer together and allowed them to quickly apply strategies taught in class in a meaningful and productive way. This prayer book is a symbol of what God's people can do when they focus on ministry and work toward one common unselfish goal. This experience was a very proud moment for me and I am grateful to God for it. I am extraordinarily proud to be the pastor of the members of DHCC and thoroughly enjoyed teaching the courses offered during each Life Application Class. I enjoy worshipping God on Sundays, Tuesdays and Wednesdays in our church and look forward to watching the members of

Destiny House continue to develop intimate relationships with God and with one another. I pray these prayers bless your lives as they did ours.

DESTINY HOUSE
CHRISTIAN CENTER

DEBT FORGIVENESS PRAYER

By: Dr. Pepper Martin

Father, we adore you for being God. We honor your presence, even, in the midst of our situation. We give you glory for being the God of provision, prosperity and purpose. Thank you that you are also the God of forgiveness, wisdom, knowledge, grace and deliverance.

We confess that we have misused our wealth. We have made foolish decisions to overspend, sow seed in infertile ground and/or without the cheerfulness that you have instructed us to have when we give.

We have signed contracts without first consulting you in prayer, committed ourselves to unethical relationships, get-rich quick schemes and co-signed for people not worthy of the use of our name or trust.

Forgive us Father for the lack of wisdom, knowledge and for not being a good steward. We have often moved in our flesh, chasing false dreams, following the lust of worldly and material possessions, and other times, being compelled by frustration.

Our frustration has not improved what we attempted to correct and often made our circumstances worse than its original state. Forgive us Father. We humbly accept your consequence for our ignorance and human error.

Help us in our frail and weak state. Help us to learn valuable lessons and never repeat them again. Help us to accept responsibility and our contribution to our condition. We acknowledge there is only One Lord, One Faith and One Baptism and You are it!

We thank you for being Lord, Savior and Advocate. According to Deuteronomy 15:1:, your word declares that, "At the end of every seven years thou shalt make a release." Release us from the offense of our ways and turn this situation around oh Lord!

You said that all things work together for the good to them that love you and are called for your purpose. We love you and are called to fulfill a divine purpose and so, Lord, we declare, by the supernatural power of the Father, in Jesus name, that this situation be annihilated by the power of the blood of Jesus! Colossians 2:14 states: 14 "Blotting out the handwriting of ordinances that was against us, which was contrary to us, and took it out of the way, nailing it to his cross." Therefore Lord, superimpose your authority over Satan's and take control in Jesus' name!

We thank you for a financial breakthrough by faith and command faith to replace fear. No weapon formed against us shall prosper, so we thank you, in advance, for being Jehovah Jireh, our provider. We thank you for the grace and stamina to destroy the negative residue left in our mind, spirit and emotions as a result of this badly incurred debt and pray for debt forgiveness, in Jesus' name.

We make our supplications known that we need a supernatural breakthrough allowing your will for our life to come into existence anyway, despite our poor decisions, ignorance and/or lack of faith. We are not God, but we serve a forgiving, loving and restoring God. Pay this bill in Jesus' name. Provide our needs and give us the strength to avoid and resist the temptation of ever repeating this cycle of failure and poverty again.

We come against generational curses and replace it with generational blessings to be lenders and not borrowers, so we don't have to be servants to lenders according to Proverbs 22:7. We will owe no one anything else, ever again, according to Romans 13:8, and by faith, we declare that debt forgiveness come by the wind of God and break ever chain of bondage in Jesus' name.

Thank you for being a debt forgiving God as you demonstrated when you shed your blood for all mankind on the cross.

"Forgive us our debts, as we forgive our debtors," according to Matthew 6:12, and grant us the grace to circumvent, undermine and destroy the demon of pride, so we can be free to receive reconciliation and restoration, as a kingdom citizen, in Jesus' name – AMEN!

PRAYER OF GOD'S PROVISION

By: Michael Robinson, Nina Daniels, Bejai Livingston and Nicole Pascal

God of Heaven and Earth, creator of all things. Hallowed is your name.

I praise you because you are a loving God. Your nature is love. I give you my praise and adoration because you are also faithful. I praise you for you are a gracious and merciful God. You are a mighty rock, my refuge. I bless you for you are patient with your children, not willing that any of us should perish but we all should repent. I praise you because you are a personal God who gives me the honor of knowing you personally just like you did for Abraham, Isaac and Jacob according to Matthews 8:11. I bless you for your goodness, mercy and grace that you give daily. I thank you for the breath that you provide that flows from you to me and gives me life. Lord, because of you I live, move and breathe. All that sustains my existence in this world is possible because of you. There is no other God above or greater than you, and I honor you in all of your majesty. Since you are my savior, I am forgiven. When I sin, and fall short of your glory, your mercy restores and covers me. When death comes to rob, steal and destroy the gifts and treasures that you give for the fullness of my soul, you confirm, in Proverbs 10:22, that "The blessings of the Lord make a person rich, and he adds no sorrow with it." You are the same God who takes care of me and promised that you will supply all my needs from your glorious riches, which have been given to all of us in Christ Jesus.

Lord, I confess with my mouth and believe with my heart that you are the Lord who provides my every need, from the rising of the sun to the settling of the same. According to Psalm 33:13, "From heaven the Lord looks down and sees all mankind; therefore, I confess that every knee shall bow and every tongue shall confess that you are Lord. The righteous shall never be forsaken nor his seed begging for bread because you are our provider and you provide for those who diligently seek you. I acknowledge my faults to you and confess that today is the dawning of a new day in my life. I confess that you are mindful of my distress and will not withhold any good thing from me. I confess you are my redeemer and you will bless me daily. I confess where ever I rest my feet it will be blessed and where I put my hands it will be blessed. I confess divine healing over my body and home. I confess that I have a focused mind. I confess prosperity and great peace in my home. As I do this, forgive me Lord, for the time I was not mindful of you and would lean on my own abilities, understanding, and the hand of men, instead of acknowledging you first, and seeking your direction and wisdom. Forgive me for not trusting you with my whole heart.

You said your word is a lamp unto our feet and a light unto our path. You have always been my compass and tour guide through life. You have always been there for me, and for that I say thank you! Thank you for being Jehovah Jireh, God my provider. You supply all of our needs. Lord you said ask and it shall be given, seek, and you shall find, knock and the door shall be opened unto you. Therefore, I ask that you to provide me with the things I need to take care of my family, my business, and Your house. Provide the finances I need, the strategies I need, the love, obedience and faith I need to see the manifestation of your promise. This is the confidence that I have in you. Lord, I believe, that if I ask anything according to your will, you will hear me and respond. I demonstrate my faith by believing and stating your word. Your word says he that comes to God must believe that He is, and that He is a rewarder of them that diligently seek Him; therefore, I thank you in advance for providing all of my needs, and doing exceedingly, abundantly above all that we ask or think according to the power that works in us and for us.

Father, there is absolutely nothing that is too hard for you. Matthew 6:26 lets us know that you are a loving father, and just as you care for the birds of the air, you will care much more for me as your child. Although life's daily obstacles at times challenge my faith, I will not be shaken. Your record with me proves that you have always been there for me and will always be with me. Father you know exactly what I need and are attentive to everything in my life. Today I let go of fear and firmly grab hold of faith. Today, I boldly accept you as the God of provision in my life, knowing there is no lack in you and therefore, there will be no lack in my life! Father, today my faith rises, and I declare, in the name of the Lord Jesus Christ, that I am a lender and not a borrower, the head and not the tail, above and not beneath. Today is the beginning of a new season in my life where I walk in increase. I thank you that everything connected to me is shifting for the better. I declare the days of drought and famine are over in my life and I walk in the abundance of God. The favor of God is my portion and today as I submit my life and my will to yours. I declare that I will prosper and be in good health even as my soul prospers. Thank you Father that things are changing for the better. Keep me from repeating the same mistakes that held me in lack and grant the wisdom needed for sustainable wealth and prosperity. You can do all things but fail, therefore, I look to you as the sustainer of my life. God, as my provider, I declare divine provision for my home, my family, my place of worship, my business, my career, my neighbors and my community. I pray that wisdom and faith will continue to work jointly in my life empowering me to seize fresh and healthy opportunities that will yield perpetual increase enabling me to be a blessing to those in need.

I thank you for being my shepherd; therefore, I shall not want, need or lack anything. In Jesus name,

Amen

PRAYER ON FINANCIAL RESPONSIBILITY

By: Joseph N. Browne, Tracy Lewis, Paula Varner and William Varner

We acknowledge God our Father, the Father of all creation; you are awesome in all your ways. We praise you for who you are, as the author and finisher of our Faith. We acknowledge you through Deut. 8:18, "But thou shalt remember the LORD thy God: for it is he that giveth thee power to get wealth, that he may establish his covenant which he sware unto thy fathers, as it is this day."

(KJV)

Father, in the Name of Jesus, please forgive us for not properly managing our finances. Thank you for another chance to change our financial responsibility, so that our families may benefit from our choices to invest and save. Lord, forgive us for every instance where we did not properly honor you with our finances. Please forgive us if we can be declared guilty by your word for:

- Unwise spending habits, in accordance to Prov. 21:20.

- Not properly honoring you through regular tithing/offering.

- Not rending to the government what was rightful regarding paying proper taxes, in accordance to your word (Matt 22:15, 22; Mark 12: 14 – 17; Luke 20: 21-26), even if our government did egregious things towards its' own citizens under the guise of legitimacy through our flawed legal system.

- Unreliable and inconsistent worship to you in our finances.

Forgive us for not exercising financial responsibility on a daily basis. Forgive us for not teaching money management to our children, so that they may pass it on to future generations. Your word states that a good man leaves an inheritance to his children's children; therefore, forgive us for being selfish, and not preparing for the future generation's financial security.

Dear Lord, thank you for your divine revelation declaring the necessity and purpose for financial accountability. We thank you for being very concerned about every facet of our life, which includes financial stability and increase. We also thank you for the charge, in accordance to your Holy Word, to always acknowledge you and to include you, even with regard to our finances. Thank you for the chance to change our way of thinking when it comes to our financial responsibility. We thank you for your charge to us to now be wise with all of the finances you have allowed us to acquire. We thank you for the shift in our thinking, the shift in our actions and the shift in our spending habits, in the name of Jesus! We further thank you for making us aware of the economic times that we presently live in. Thank you for making us aware of our personal poor financial choices and the poor financial choices made by our governmental systems. We repent before you. The future of global economic decisions dictate the need to intentionally prepare against the threat of the enemy overtaking us through financial disaster, and immediately plan for the future, and for that, we say thank you!

Dear Lord, we pray for the renewing of our mind; we pray for divine order in our financial planning. Free us from the bondage of unnecessary spending.   We further pray for your charge regarding consistent responsibility over our finances, which include consistently paying all of our bills on time, and not accruing unnecessary debt. We came against the temptation of overspending on credit/charge cards, store cards, making payday and quick cash loans, unnecessary ATM use, and using check cashing places as our primary banking sources. We want to be trustworthy with every dime, every nickel and every penny that you have allowed us to receive, for Luke 16:11 tells us plainly, "and if you are untrustworthy about worldly wealth, who will trust you with the true riches of heaven?"(KJV) We want to be prudent with what you have allowed us to gain through employment, or running businesses through legitimate entrepreneurship, and even through previously unplanned means of monetary gain (such as a financial inheritance) by exercising the principle of seed time and harvest, as well as regular giving to our local church, which includes both regular offering and regular tithing.

As we ask for your guidance, we commit to your word that tells us the wise have wealth and luxury, but fools spend whatever they get (Prov. 21:20). We pray that we can invest and save to provide a better life for our children, and that we are lenders and not borrowers. If we fail to plan, we cannot be free from the god of materialism, and the means of protection against the waste of resources you have entrusted to us. Luke 14:28 says "Suppose one of you wants to build a tower. Won't you first sit down and estimate the cost to see if you have enough money to complete it?" (NIV)

Lord, help us to properly prepare NOW. Help us to completely overhaul our financial behavior that will honor you appropriately. Teach us how to fully worship you with all of our finances. Help us to learn immediately how to stop spending money unnecessarily, how to save money, and also how to properly invest in the future and for the future. Help us dear Lord how to hear your voice through the Holy Spirit as to where we are to invest, how much to invest, and for how long. Let us be abundantly able to leave an inheritance to our future seed, in accordance to Prov. 13:22. Let our financial resources truly bring glory to your name; let us never be ashamed. We believe in the blessings of Abraham, and we believe in your promise of the blessings you have in store for our life. We will bless your house, bless our family, care for ourselves and bless our community for your glory in Jesus Name! AMEN.

THE GIVING PRAYER

By the Members of DHCC: Pastor Sydney Martin, Michael Anderson and Frances Dent

Heavenly Father we give you honor and glory, and praise your holy name. We thank you that the word of God is alive and active! Thank you for being holy; you are Lord and the only true God. Your deeds are wonderful. You are strong. You are great. You are the most high. You are almighty. You are our heavenly father, and King of Heaven and Earth. Lord, God you are good, all good, supremely good. You are love, wisdom and humility. You are endurance. You are a guardian and defendant. You are courage. You are our haven and our hope. You are our faith, and great consolation and our eternal hope. You are God almighty and merciful Savior. The true vine, and we are, the branch. You are the protector of our finances and wealth and for that we thank you. We love you today; you are worthy of all the praise.

We confess we have not treated you the way you have treated us. Thank you for your mercy and grace. When I robbed you of tithes and offerings and gifts and talents, you never retaliated. You returned my robbery at times with blessings because of your internal kindness, and for that, I say thank you. You've never robbed me of your love and care and never based it on anything. It was given with no strings attached and for that, I am most grateful.

We ask you today to forgive us for our daily sins. Some that we know and some unknown. We fall short today of your Glory - God. We ask for forgiveness, especially for not giving unto you, when we know of some one in need. We ask for forgiveness of a selfish heart, for we have not been faithful in our giving. We ask for forgiveness and try us one more time.

We ask you for a new mindset in serving you, God, in the spirit of giving. We acknowledge there is one God that is able to lead and guide us. Forgive us if we have robbed you of tithes and offerings, robbed you of our gifts and talents, robbed you of time and resources that we have in our arsenal. Oh god we repent, apologize and ask for forgiveness for coming up short and holding back, for not sacrificing but robbing you in our giving. Thank you for wise financial counselors, teachers and clergy who are teaching us the principles of good stewardship.

We declare and decree today that we have a change of heart and thoughts when it comes to our giving - Let us not continue to have a selfish spirit! Heavenly father, thank you for blessing us when we did not deserve it. Thank you for your grace and mercy each day. YOU ARE A WONDERFUL blessing to us and we thank you. We ask you to cover our families and friends at this time. For those who do not know you, let us be the light for them to follow in Jesus name!

The Bible says in Malachi 3:8: Will a mere mortal rob God? Yet, you robbed me. But you ask, how are we robbing you? In tithes and offerings you are under a curse your whole nation because you are robbing me. Bring the whole tithes into the storehouse, that there maybe food in my house. Test me in this, says the Lord Almighty, and see if I will not throw open the floodgates of heaven and pour out so much blessing that there will not be room enough to store it."

We thank you for revelation of this scripture. We are thanking you with all our heart and will tell of your wonderful deeds. Let us be grateful for what you have given us. Let us give from our hearts and not begrudgingly. Help us to also give of the time, talents and gifts you gave to us, so that we can use them to build up the kingdom of God.   Luke 21:1-4 MSG [1-4] Just then he looked up and saw the rich people dropping offerings in the collection plate. Then he saw a poor widow put in two pennies. He said, "The plain truth is that this widow has given by far the largest offering today. All these others made offerings that they'll never miss; she gave extravagantly what she couldn't afford---she gave her all!"

Therefore, we intercede today for others in need to be obedient to the word God has given to us. We pray today that others would realize that it is better to give than to receive. Now, God, we petition you, that we will obey your word. We use your word to give life to our situations. We speak to every stronghold, every obstacles and every challenge that we tempt us not to give and we challenge our spirit to give, to give according to your Word that our own difficult situations and the challenges for those whom we pray for will be annihilated in Jesus' name!

By delighting ourselves, in you Lord, we trust that we will be cared for by your hand. According to your Word, which instructs us to delight ourselves in you. Lord, help us to please you so that what you have given to us will enable us to continue to give to others – in Jesus name – Amen!

GREED FORGIVENESS PRAYER

By: Ann Steele, Jayson Smith, Kara Smith and Christopher Williams

Father God, we praise you with all that we are, for being who you are. You are all powerful, mighty and the one we adore. You are our source when we cannot find our own way, and even in our weakness, you rain supreme!

We stand before you to confess that we have been obsessed with accumulating material goods, often valuing materials things more than you.

This obsession is called Greed and it is a sin of addiction. Greed has tempted us many times to over-indulge ourselves where we should have exercised restraint, and as a result, we did not realize the damage and the risk of self-imposed exile where Your will for our lives has been disregarded. We have allowed our greed to become our jailor and find ourselves foolishly believing that we are the head our lives.

We have taken our blessed seed and allowed our poor choices tied up in greed to lead us astray, only to find that we were deceived. Father, we have failed to seek your guidance, and wherever we went against your will, we have found nothing but lack and heartache instead of the bountiful blessings that you promised. The bible declares in Proverbs 30:15-16 (MSG) "A leech has twin daughters named "Gimme" and "Gimme more." And so, Lord we recognize that because of our greed we are akin to leeches in your sight; therefore, we stand before you, asking for your forgiveness. Please help us, please free us from our own self-imposed bondage of greed.

Father, we have allowed our greed to become our lord and master even though we are encouraged in Hebrews 13:5 (MSG) not to be obsessed with getting more material things but to be relaxed with what we have. The same scripture continues to assure us that you will never let us down, nor ever walk off and leave us…" With great humility, we apologize for our selfish and excessive desire for more than is needed and we ask for your continued forgiveness. We have failed to trust and wait on you to supply all our needs and for allowing the distractions of Satan the deceiver to interfere with our ability to give. Our greed has often allowed us to rob you, and allowed our homes to go without. But, you promised us in Malachi 3:10 (MSG) that if we bring our full tithe to the temple treasury and test you, you will open heaven itself and bless us beyond our wildest dreams. We choose to believe your word and from this day forward will seek you first before making even the simplest of decisions.

Father we thank you for your word in Luke 12:15 (MSG) that declares "...Take care! Protect yourself against the least bit of greed. Life is not defined by what you have, even when you have a lot." Thank you Lord for allowing us to recognize greed as an addiction and we ask that it be killed at the root and replaced will an insatiable desire of faith and trust. We have chosen to plant our seed in good ground and will allow you to water it and grant the increase. You have extended mercy to us by allowing us to see the error of our ways before we caused irreversible damage to ourselves and to all connected to us. Finally, God, we choose to be good stewards with our seed. We pray that the supernatural power of God will continue to be our guide and compass, and should greed reappear, we are confident that greed will find no vacancy within us as long as we remain aligned to Your Will.

You have showed up and showed out in our lives time and time again, and for that, we thank you. You have closed doors that should never have been opened and opened new doors with access to new and awesome opportunities, and for that, we thank you.

Our supplication is that we allow your will to supersede any desires we have, fostered in greed, that prevent your perfect will from being fulfilled within our lives. We pray that generational behaviors borne out of ignorance will be replaced by 'greediness' for your word and that we will live as the bible declares in Matthew 6: 33 (KJV) "But seek ye first the kingdom of God, and his righteousness: and all these things shall be added unto you." We are encouraged also by the Message bible version of the same scripture to "Steep our life in God-reality, God-initiative, God-provisions. Don't worry about missing out. You'll find all your everyday human concerns will be met.

So, Father, thank you for your forgiveness and for opening our spiritual eyes. We also thank you for the gift of discernment so that we can recognize the tricks of the deceiver. We pray for the fortitude to stand when the enemy tries to overtake our minds, thoughts and actions and break the spirit of greediness for your honor and glory in Jesus' name. Amen

Meet the Authors

This is no ordinary prayer book, but any anointed tool designed to break spiritual strongholds on the finances of God's people! Co-authored along the side of their Pastor, Dr. Pepper Martin, the students of the Life Application Class at Destiny House Christian Center Church joined in a collaborative experience that was not only academically enriching, but also so spiritually empowering that it became a life changing event for the bible class students and later the entire congregation. What initially began as bible class assignment, turned into power-packed spiritual experience that Dr. Martin knew needed to be shared with others. This book offers powerful, heart-felt pocket prayers combining concepts from two LAC courses entitled, "Praise and Prayer Power," and "Money Matters," designed to destroy strongholds in the lives of God's people that often act as barriers to financial progress necessary to build God's kingdom seamlessly. What began a class assignment given by Dr. Pepper Martin to her students turned the drudgery of doing homework into an effective ministry tool. Therefore, Dr. Pepper Martin and the DHCC Life Application Class students pray this book acts as a guide to help you discover your road to financial freedom based on biblical principle.

www.dhcc.church

www.ingramcontent.com/pod-product-compliance
Lightning Source LLC
Chambersburg PA
CBHW032110040426
42449CB00007B/1237